YOUR BEST SECOND HALF

A Practical Guide for Men to Thrive in Life's Second Half

PETER SOER

Peter Soer | Peter@BravelyHonestlyGenerously.com

Cartoons by Mark Anderson | Andertoons.com

Cover design by KUHN Design Group | Kuhndesigngroup.com

Your Best Second Half

First edition published in 2024

ISBN: 978-1-7384-7810-1 (paperback)
ISBN: 978-1-7384-7811-8 (eBook)

For Shirley, Will, Hugo,
Anita and Frank
For Optimism, for
Determination, for Love

INTRODUCTION

WHY SHOULD YOU BELIEVE THIS?

Nature + Nurture:
The lessons of my childhood.

35+ Year Career in
Marketing and Coaching.

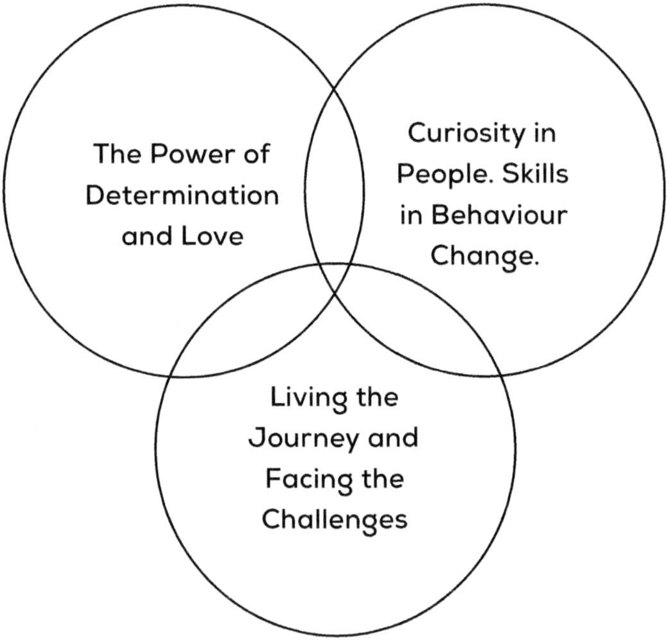

I, and my friends, and
many of my coaching clients
are living this journey.

My name is Peter Soer. I have written this book because I believe that with a few actionable coaching tools to use, men can lead more of the life they want. Yet currently, there is nothing actionable, enjoyable, or effective written for them. We have a brief time on this planet, so let's live it to the full. Why should you believe what I have to say? Three aspects of my life make me uniquely qualified.

1) Nature + Nurture:
The power of determination and love.

Both of my parents faced significant life adversity. This forged in them a great determination and with my mother, a great capacity to love. Through their genes and their raising me, I learnt the power of determination and love.

My mother, Anita, was born in Germany before World War II. She watched her family shop being destroyed by the Nazis and her father being beaten. She left Germany in 1939 at age ten and came to the UK. My mother and her siblings arrived without their parents. They never saw them again. Later they were to find out they perished in a concentration camp.

My father, Frank, was one of four children, born into a hard-working East London family. Many children were evacuated from London to escape the war bombing. In 1940, at the age of fourteen, Frank was evacuated to South Africa, a completely foreign land for him. While there, he had to deal with the destabilisation of moving a number of times between families who gave him a place to stay, and he was badly bullied at school.

Frank and Anita met in Sheffield, UK and married in 1953. They faced many ups and downs in life but stayed together. They are both dead now. They lost their first child to pneumonia at the age of three weeks and went on to have two more children. My sister Daphne and me.

They created a safe, stable home for us. My mother brought love and kindness. My father brought analytical curiosity and planning. They both embodied duty, determination, and a belief that life could be better.

I have a pronounced spinal curve—scoliosis. You might have seen older people standing bent over, almost looking at the floor—that can be the result of scoliosis.

I suffer daily pain, and my scoliosis torso contributes to my lack of physical confidence. However, through daily focused exercise and determination, I have limited the spinal curvature, and I manage the pain. I know that many people have much worse physical challenges than this, but this is the one I have to deal with, and I do.

2) A 35+ year career in Marketing and Coaching. Curiosity in people and skills in behaviour change.

I worked for almost thirty years in marketing-led businesses, ultimately leading teams diverse in gender, nationality, culture, religion and age. These roles nurtured in me a deep curiosity about people, and how and why they behave. It taught me how to communicate, to simplify, to illuminate.

I am British. I had the good fortune to live and work both in the UK and outside of my home culture—in China, the Netherlands and Ireland. During these years, I was able to experience and understand what it is like to be in the minority. This gives me extra perspective and empathy.

Since 2016, I have been a coach, working with people to bring out their capability within themselves, articulate and achieve their goals, and live more of the life they want. I learn with every client and every new approach and work with several peer groups of nurturing wonderful coaches. Almost 2000 hours of coaching so far, and still going strong. The core of coaching is enabling people to achieve their goals through changes in their mindset and behaviours.

3) I am a 'Life's second half man', living the journey, facing the challenges—myself, my friends, many of my clients.

The world is flooded with 'self-help', 'health & wellness', 'live a better life' books, and yet none of them that I have seen are written from the perspective of a mature man, for mature men. I believe that my living this journey enables me to write a guide that is actually designed for 'life's second half men'.

In my mid-40s, moving into a big promotion triggered imposter feelings—'I am not enough for this role. I am going to be found out'.

My initial solution was to work ever harder and longer, which, of course, led to my performance getting worse rather than better and had a negative impact on my colleagues. I was very fortunate to receive professional coaching, which helped me to understand my imposter voices, make them quieter, and harness my strengths instead. As a result, I succeeded in my promoted role and led business growth of +50% over 5 years.

My cousin Bernie and close friend Roger each took their lives. Such a terrible waste. Wonderful human beings with so much still to live, love, give and receive. This left me feeling (a) how important it is for people to be able to talk about life's challenges rather than keeping stuff bottled up inside and (b) how precious is our short time alive, so make the best of it we possibly can.

I have made many mistakes, missed opportunities, and been selfish and clumsy.

I have loved, tried to turn up when I am needed, and tried to bring positive energy.

I am a pragmatic optimist. I believe that life can be better. This stuff doesn't have to be complex. Equally, it isn't easy.

But with motivation and some practical tools, you can make the shifts you want to make.

I am husband to Shirley, father to Will and Hugo. I have learnt from each of them from the day we met, and continue to do so. Most powerfully, how to love and be loved. Being a father to Will and Hugo is the greatest joy and privilege of my life.

I believe that life is not a test. It is a non-stop opportunity to learn. When we live with this mindset, we try out new things, we grow in confidence, and we shine positive energy for ourselves and those around us.

So, now you know a little more about me, let's get back to this guide. I simply want you to get the best you can from your remaining years on this planet—for you, yourself and for the positive ripple effect you will have on everyone you know. I believe for most of us, this journey does not require therapy or a retreat with a life transformation guru. It takes an open mind to try out new ways of thinking and behaviours, determination and some courage. We are all different, so there is no magic formula, but you can choose the tools in this guide that feel best for you, and they will work.

You may be asking what or when life's second half is? I believe it is not a specific age. It begins with the moment in life when you ask the *is this it?* question of yourself. For many, it is somewhere between 30 and 60 years old.

Peter Soer 2023

CONTENTS

Step 1: Get started

Step 2: Open your mind

Step 3: See your possibility

Step 4: Learn from how you got here

Step 5: Make small changes and get big differences

Step 6: Refresh your key relationships

STEP 1

GET STARTED

IS THIS IT!?
Next 20 Years

(1.1) Why do you need this book?

Because too many men enter life's second half, wake up one day and ask this question…

"Is this it?!"

Or something similar, and have nowhere useful to go to work out the answer.

The cards are stacked against you because many of the unwritten rules for men are obstacles preventing you from finding answers:

- be strong
- people don't change
- suck it up, stop whinging and get on with it

And weirdly, none of your friends seems to need to talk, so you are left thinking *it must just be me overthinking stuff*. So, instead of finding a way to think things through, you go for a pint or a run or walk the dog or do something useful instead.

The result is that for your remaining decades, you accept a life that is *okay* rather than the best it can be, wasting some of your life's second-half opportunity.

Then one day, twenty or thirty years later, you awake to a new question.

'Was that what I wanted?'

But by that point, it is too late to do much about it. The opportunity you had to have the best possible second half has gone.

It doesn't have to be like that. With a few actionable tools, you can have more of the life you want.

That is where this book comes in. If you are curious whether the rest of your life can hold greater possibilities and more potential and how you can make it happen, then this is for you.

You don't have to face a crisis for this guide to be for you. This guide is useful if you would simply like your years ahead to be the best they can be.

(1.2) What is this book and how to use it?

This book is a simple, actionable guide to help you do more than just get through life's second half. To help you realise that, far from having to just keep going, you have great potential, combining experience of the past with energy for the future.

Only you own the pen that writes the story of your life.

The core tools I will use are questions and exercises which ask you to think, write, and reflect. The questions are specifically designed to enable people to see with fresh eyes, to generate new understanding, and to unlock their potential as valuable human beings.

Get a pen and some paper, or a notebook, or your favourite device to type with. You will be thinking and writing/typing your thoughts. The guide helps you to do the thinking in bite-size steps, with each step building on the last, so

Unwritten
Rules of
Manhood

that by the end, you will have new insight, clear choices and actionable plans to get what you want out of life's second half.

Many books feel like they are three ideas stretched into three hundred pages. My aim with this guide is the opposite—it is short and power-packed. Don't rush. Give yourself time between exercises to let your unconscious explore and build on the thoughts you had. You will likely want to come back to your work and add thoughts and ideas to it.

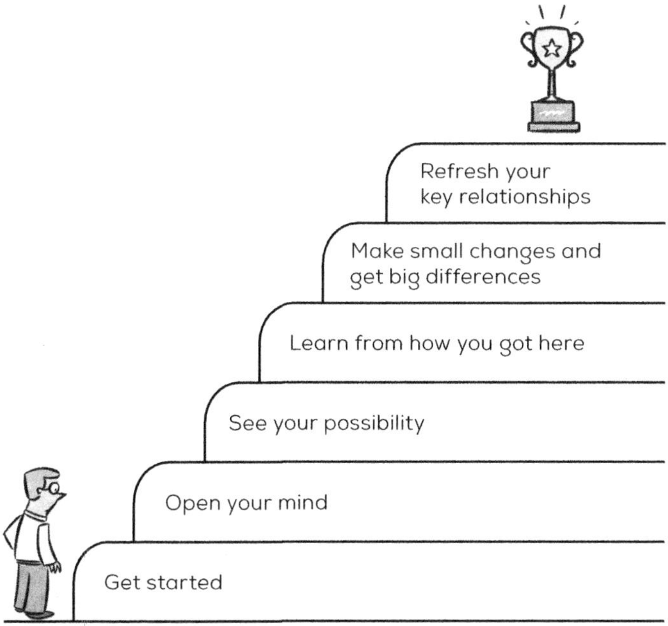

(1.3) What happens if you read on?

This guide is structured like a conversation. I hope you will find it easy and enjoyable to read.

You will find insights that you can action, torch lights that switch on and help you see a new way ahead, generating optimistic energy that you can harness. The guide provides language and questions you can use with your family and friends to open up new discussions that will help you and help them.

We are all different, and so you and the guy sitting next to you will each find the most value in different parts of this book. For sure, there is something in here that will work for you… a life 10% better, a relationship improved, an opportunity uncovered. With each step forward, you gain momentum, and it becomes clear that you do not have to accept that *this is it.*

So, mindful of two of my favourite quotes:

> *"Whether you think you can, or you think you can't, you're right."*
>
> HENRY FORD

"Unless you believe the future can be better, you are unlikely to step up and take responsibility for making it so."

NOAM CHOMSKY

Come along, let's have some fun.

STEP 2

OPEN YOUR MIND

"OK so you've got work from 9:00 to 11:00, working harder 11:00 to 2:00, working even harder 2:00 to 6:00, and then exhaustion From 6:00 on."

In this short step, we start to open the mind with a conversation and a story.

(2.1) Is this it?

"Is this it?"

Is what what?

"Is this how my life should be now?

How is your life now?

"It's fine… It's good… I am very lucky…

It's just… it's just…

I am not sure if I am doing what I want to do anymore.

Maybe I haven't been for years, but it didn't seem to matter before, as I was so busy with the work, children, the house, getting stuff done, squeezing in some fun now and then. But now, something feels different, and I am not sure what I should be doing."

Who decides what you should be doing with your life now?

"The need to pay the bills, to keep my job, keep my relationship together, on track, be a good dad now/one day… and what else, what else? I suppose… my parents—there is still a part of me that wants to please them, that wants them to be proud of me. Everyone, everything out there, decides what I should be doing… I can't get off the wheel. I just have to keep pedalling in order to stand still. And anyway, if I wasn't busy doing what I am supposed to do, what else would I do?"

Really, so everyone and everything else decides what you should do with your life now?

Frowns

"Oh, FFS, are you going to keep asking until I say… Me?"

And is it really about what you should be doing or what you

want to be doing? The problem with *should* is that it usually means the expectations of others—parents, alive or dead, partners, friends, colleagues, society. And somehow, early in life, you absorbed all these *shoulds*, and didn't question them too hard. It got you to where you are now, and that's fine. But now, you can stop living on *auto-should*, and instead choose what you want to do.

So what do you want?

"I don't know!"

(2.2) What do you want?

So what do you want?

"To...

have more flexibility in my life
have more choices
do different work, feel more excited about my work
enjoy more sex, different sex, better sex
not worry about money
not wake up feeling anxious

spend more time with my dad
drink less alcohol
get back to playing in my local football side again
lose some weight, feel fitter
do some charity work, do something to give back a little
worry less about my children
be able to talk about stuff with my partner
be able to talk about stuff with my friends
be able to talk about stuff with someone
feel more purpose in my life"

Wow

You will recognise some of these, not all, and you will have others.

Just by starting to articulate this stuff and hearing the words come out of your mouth, things start to move, and possibilities start to show themselves. These *wants* are very typical for men in life's second half. You may have one, some, many wants. They may seem to fit together or be at odds with each other. Each of them can be worked through, and life-affirming momentum gained.

(2.3) In this next phase of your life, what is important to you?

In this next phase of your life, what is important to you?

"Isn't that just the same as what do I want?!"

It may seem that way at first, but it digs deeper. It takes you into motivations and values. It is one of the best questions. When you answer it simply and honestly, all sorts of things start to become clearer. It is much better than *what motivates you?* or *what are your values?* because those questions often drive people into giving esoteric answers or answering with what they think they *should* say.

(2.4) "The story of the Mexican Fisherman"*

Once upon a time, a New York businessman (BM) was travelling in Mexico. He had a free morning. It was a beautiful sunny day by the sea, and so when he saw the chance to go out on a small fishing boat with a local tuna fisherman (FM), he went along.

* This story is an adaptation from the wonderful original "The Story of the Mexican Fisherman" by Courtney Carver. You can find that original and other great work by Courtney Carver at the website bemorewithless.com

They had a lovely morning out on the water. The fisherman caught two tuna and then sailed the boat back to land at around lunchtime.

BM: Thank you for a lovely morning. I hope you don't mind me asking, but I wonder what are you going to do with the rest of your day?

FM: Of course not. Feel free. I am going to sell these two tuna fish. Then I am going home to have lunch with my wife. We will make love this afternoon and have some rest. The children will come home later, and after they do some homework, we will all eat together and then maybe go for a walk on the beach or play some games or sit and chat and laugh until it is time to wash and sleep.

BM: Oh, I see. Thank you. It is just… I was just wondering… Well, you caught these two fish this morning quite quickly and easily… so I was wondering if you could go back out in the afternoon and catch two more and then sell them too?

FM: Well, yes, I suppose I could. But why would I do that?

BM: Well, if you do that, you can save the money that you

earn from the extra two fish, and after a few weeks, you could buy a second boat.

FM: Interesting, yes I see, and what would I do with another boat?

BM: You can employ another fisherman to go fishing with that boat and double the money that you make each day. And once you have done that for a few weeks, you will have enough money to buy another boat and another boat until you have a small fleet of fishing boats working from this village and perhaps other villages up the coast.

FM: And what would that mean for me?

BM: Well, you would have to work more than you are working now, as there will be things to organise, but you will make a lot of money, and maybe you could buy yourself a bigger house and a nice car. And then, of course, with this success, you would be able to invest in your own canning factory. Why let someone else have the profit of preparing the tuna, putting it in cans, and selling it to the shops?! Much better that you do that too.

FM: Well, I don't know anything about factories, but I guess I could learn.

BM: Sure, and you can employ good people who know about factories. It will take some time and hard work, maybe a few years, say five years, but then you could have the local fishing fleet and the canning factory, and you will be an important person in this town.

FM: An important person, hey… how about that.that?

BM: Then, once you know how to do it here, in this area, you can repeat it all the way up the coast of this region. Eat up the competition and set the prices. Probably to do that, it will be best for you to move to Mexico City or even New York City—that is where the investments and the real skills are, so it is much easier to run a big growing business there. It might take 10-15 years to get to that phase. But wow, tuna is a great business, and you will be rich.

FM: And how would be my life in New York all this time?

BM: Super busy, doing business there and coming back here sometimes to ensure everything is going well. Your children can go to a great school, and your wife and you will have a lovely home and car and clothes, everything you want.

FM: Sounds like I will be very busy, and very successful. When I have done all this, in 20-25 years' time, what will I do?

BM: Well, you will probably want some time for yourself. So maybe you would find a quiet place near the beach, go fishing in the morning, have lunch with your wife and make love in the afternoon. If you are lucky, maybe your children will come and visit you occasionally so you can share a meal with them and your grandchildren and go for a walk on the beach together.

Think: What does this story tell you?

This story is a reminder that much of society tells us that what we should do is work harder, go higher, earn more, have more. And yet, the things we really want are often the simple things in life which we can have without losing ourselves on that path.

STEP 3

SEE YOUR POSSIBILITY

On this journey, it is important to write/type stuff. The mere action of putting stuff into your own words and letting it come down your arms and hands onto paper or keyboard starts to change how you think and feel.

In this step, you will answer a number of questions and do several exercises. Give yourself time. You don't have to do all of this stage in one sitting. Just do the exercises one by one and reflect in between. They build one on the other to unlock your understanding and thinking.

So take a pen and some paper, or a notebook, or your favourite device to type onto.

(3.1) How is my life now?

Answer this question—How is my life now?

Just write… anything… words, thoughts, feelings, sentences. And/or draw if that works for you. A list, a paragraph, a mind map, Anything. Don't edit, don't try to make it make sense. Just let it come out. The good things, the great things, the things you wish could be more or less or different. Think across all and any aspects of your life—home, family, friends, work, community, pastimes, hobbies, passions.

(3.2) What do I want?

Answer this question—What do I want?

You guessed it:

Just write… anything… words, thoughts, feelings, sentences. And/or draw if that works for you. A list, a paragraph, a mind map… anything. Don't edit, don't try to make it make sense. Just let it come out. Think broadly—for yourself, your family members, your close friends, maybe your community. Include stuff that may seem small e.g. *to start playing local football again*, and stuff that feels big like *bring some of the early romance with my partner back into our relationship now* or *make a bigger contribution to reduce climate change*. This is about freeing up your thoughts and feelings. When you think about what you want, it is most useful if you can see how you can have an effect on the *want*, rather than *dreams* which are fully dependent on other people.

(3.3) Don't put up with should

It is possible that when you are writing, you find yourself thinking about what you should do, be, want. Should is a dangerous thing. It usually comes from someone else in our life or perhaps just some nebulous belief that somehow got planted in your head. The more you can puncture the should in how you think about life, the better.

A tactic for *should*:

Every time you hear, read or say *should*, stop and ask:

'Who says?'

'Why?'

'Does this *should* fit with what I want?'

MAP
You're
Still
Here?!

(3.4) Wherever I go, there I am

A part of you feels like the world needs to change or other people have to change for things to be how you want them to be. Or that if only you could change job or house or partner, then your life would be better. The problem with this part of your thinking is that *wherever you go, there you are.* What does that mean? Simply, even if you change some aspect of your context/external life, after an initial period of excitement/new hope, things will tend to revert to how they felt before. You will start to have the same non-ideal feelings. Why is it like this? Why can't you progress in your job the way you want? Why is your new partner also not being how you want them to be? This is because you are still the same. So, you have to change the way you think, the things you do, the way you make choices, your ability to be intentional, and then your life will change. You may not need to change job, or house, or partner at all. You may simply need to change some mindsets and behaviours.

Increased confidence comes from taking actions slightly beyond your comfort zone. It may sound scary, but it is the best way. You don't become confident and then be able to do new stuff. You have to do some of the new stuff, realise that you can (it may take a few goes, that's fine), and then you feel more confident.

Using this guide, you are going to be intentional. You will set your direction, make plans and commit to actions. Some of these intentions and actions will feel beyond your current comfort zone. That is good. You will achieve them, and that will bring you more confidence and energy.

(3.5) Own your own achievements and powers.

Create a list of your achievements large and small—and specifically what you did to land that achievement.

Write down a list of your accomplishments (A) and for each one, what you did to land that achievement (WID)—not *I was lucky*. e.g.

A: I got decent grades in my school exams.

WID: Planned my revision and stuck to the plan. Resisted the temptation to go out with my mates.

A: After 50 applications, I finally got a good job after college.

WID: Asked my uncle for help practise for interviews. Didn't get discouraged when I got no replies to my applications. Ensured that I always turned up on time and looked good for interviews. Kept learning from each application and interview how I could do better. Kept my head up. Believed in myself.

A: I ran a marathon.

WID: Researched trainers and bought some real running shoes. Read a lot about how to run. Planned my training and stuck to it. I was determined and organised. I stretched myself further than I thought I could.

A: Decorated my apartment while living in it with my partner and still managed to get on well.

WID: I stayed calm and focused on what I love about her when she is annoying me. When I felt frustrated, I breathed deeply and counted to five before saying anything. I let myself have a view on how it would look, even though I have never felt or been encouraged to be 'arty'.

A: Organised a great holiday for me and my family.

WID: I did lots of research. I planned ahead. I asked what people would like, and then I made a judgement on balance of the various views.

A: Turned up for my friend when his mum died.

WID: I prioritised friendship. I told my boss I needed the time off. I just turned up and was with him, calmly, being, not fussing.

A: Sang in the local choir.

WID: It was brave of me to try it, and it turned out I can sing.

A: Got promoted twice at work and am now a director.

WID: I focussed on the key deliverables of my role, I had tough discussions with team members, I led the creation of a great business plan, and I presented it to the Board.

Do this over a few sessions. Take your time. Don't sift. Write down achievements, large and small. It is all useful. Then,

"It says here under Accomplishments
'Put up with my brother-in-law Stephen.'
Tell me about that..."

read through and look for patterns in what you did. Write a list of these patterns/common factors. This will give you clues to some of your strengths/powers. From the example above, that person might see determination, hard work, turning up to help others when they need it, researching problems, asking for help, staying calm under pressure. Now think how you can use these personal powers more in the years ahead. How can you use them to make it happen for the things that are important to you? Use the strengths you have identified.

See Appendix 1 for an example.

(3.6) In this next phase of my life, what is important to me?

This tool takes a bit more engineering.

Get some Post-it notes and a pen, and answer the question. In this next phase of my life, what is important to me?

Write one discrete answer per Post-it note. Each answer is more than a word and less than a sentence.

Some examples:

- Spend at least one hour a day with my children while they are still young
- Earn a minimum of £xyz for ten years
- Have more fun romantic times with my wife e.g. date night once a week
- Find a new job with more creative content
- Be able to stay living in our current house
- Work for a company that really believes in inclusivity & the environment
- Make time for fitness—run three times a week
- Make time to see my parents once a month
- Spend time with my friends, not drinking alcohol, e.g. walk the dogs together twice a week
- Study part-time
- Stay in my current company, but get a different job with less client work

- Write a book
- Give 2 hours a week of my time to a local charity
- Get an allotment and learn how to grow vegetables

The answers are apples and pears, and some of them may seem to conflict with each other. Some will seem big and some small. That is good. First time around, you will probably come up with more than ten and less than twenty. You will already be doing some of these things, a lot or little, and some of these things may be new thoughts.

Once you have a small pile of Post-it notes, then you can force rank them.

Pick up any two Post-it notes, look at them/read them out, and decide which of these two is more important. Put them on the table in front of you, the more important one above (further away from you than) the other… you are starting to make a column.

Take a third Post-it. Read it, and ask yourself, is it more important than the first or second? If it is less important than the first and more important than the second, then put it in between the first two Post-it notes. And then a fourth, and so on… You will have to keep moving the Post-it notes to make space.

Because the answers are apples and pears, it can feel hard to rank them. And you may want to put Post-it notes next to each other—equal ranking. Don't! Make yourself rank above and below. And don't be tempted to game it—Ah now I know how this works, I will put things in the order that fits with what I have done, am doing, or I know I should do!

No, no, no. The whole point is to open up your real thinking as it is now.

Once you have your column of what is important, sit back and look at it. What does it tell you? Is it what you expected? In particular, what are your top four or six? These are the things you need to put energy into in the time ahead. Are there things that you thought were important to you but have actually ended up quite low down? That is really helpful. Maybe they have been distractions or have even got in the way—stopped you doing things that are more important. Now you know, so you can deprioritise them, at least in this next phase of life.

Your time and our resources are finite, so you are constantly making choices about how to use them. This tool helps you to start to see what is really important to you. When you have your list, this helps you to prioritise where to put your energy (time and resources) for change. And it gives you criteria, a lens through which to appraise new options when they arise, e.g. a new job opportunity or a chance to move house.

Number the Post-it notes, and then type them up into a table or list so you don't lose them. You may well change the order over time or on reflection. That's fine. This is a great start.

Now, turn your *What is Important to Me* list into priorities for action

Come back to your list in a few days. Read through it. Is it still about right, or now you have done more thinking, do you need to add anything or change the order? Then, take the top five items one by one. For the first item:

- Are you doing enough to make this happen?
- What needs to change?

- What is getting in the way? How to reduce that barrier?
- Who can help? What can help?

» Make your plan

Then do the same for item two.

Some of the items may well be fully underway and resourced. Great, tick and move on. This exercise is to help you ensure that you are devoting your time, energy and resources e.g. money, to the things that are important to you.

This list will also change over time. e.g. if you do the exercise again in five years, you may have some different items and/or a different order. That is fine.

See Appendix 1 for an example.

"Well, John, if I'm to believe Señor Stegosaurus, it sounds like maybe instead of accounting, you'd prefer to pursue a career in puppetry?"

(3.7) The most important letter you can write now ... to yourself

Imagine it is twenty years from today, and you are writing down how the last twenty years have been—what do you want to be able to write?

The tools so far have loosened things up in your head and heart. You have started to shed the *shoulds*, and instead look at what you want and is important to you. Now, this tool gives you the opportunity to write your own story for your life's second half.

Imagine the moment, see it, feel it. Maybe it is in twenty years' time or thirty, you decide. Where are you sitting? Is anyone else there? What can you see, feel, smell?

Be honest with yourself—say it, write it, feel it. How do you want that time to have been? Who have you spent time with? What did you do? What did you not do? What brought you happiness? To whom did you bring happiness, support, and love? Who have you been?

What was important to you? What could get in the way of you being this person in this letter, and so how can you remove those barriers before they get in the way?

Sometimes, you dare not say what you really hope for. You think that maybe you can't have it, that maybe it is not possible, and so why hope and then be disappointed? There are two key answers to this:

If you tell yourself and the world what you want, there is a much bigger chance that you will get it. It is amazing what people will do to help, and how suddenly, just by shifting your thoughts, new possibilities show themselves.

> *"You can choose to live disappointment or to risk feeling disappointment."*
>
> BRENÉ BROWN

I suggest you take the risk.

See Appendix 1 for an example.

Take your *most important letter*—read it, really read it, feel it

Now you know how you want life's second half to be. To be able to write this letter when the time comes, what shifts do you need to make now and in the months and years ahead?

Some will already be covered by the decisions you made in step (3.6), just now. There will also be other stuff that needs to happen. For example, who do you need to talk with more, or less or in a different way? This exercise has probably made you think longer term. So for example, *what is important to me in the next phase of my life* may have focussed on career, family, close friends and health. In the years after that, maybe other things will be important—rediscovering your joy for travel or gardening, putting time into the community, caring for grandchildren. Sometimes, people discover from their letter that relationships are even more important than they thought, and possessions and career achievements are less important.

(3.8) Use your possibility building blocks to build your plan

'How is my life now' got you thinking.

'What do I want?' enabled you to open your mind in ways you otherwise might not do and capture your thoughts and feelings.

'In this next phase of my life, what is important to me' pushed your rational brain to be specific about what really is important in the coming years.

The *most important letter* released your emotional brain to see and feel the stuff that really matters in life's second half.

'Own your achievements and powers' helped you to see your strengths/powers, which you can use to help you live the life you want.

Now you have key building blocks of how you want your life's second half to be. You have written them or typed them. You have the core of your plan to go forward. Use the actions coming from 'What is important to me' as the basis for the weeks, months and perhaps one to five years ahead. From your *most important letter* add in anything more or perhaps cut out something that really isn't as important as you thought. Keep your list of strengths and look at it every few weeks to remind yourself to use your powers to live the life you want. Perhaps you can add into some of your actions how you will use your strengths to get the outcomes you want.

Don't try to do everything. Focus on the top priorities. Perhaps do some phasing—start some things now and others in a year.

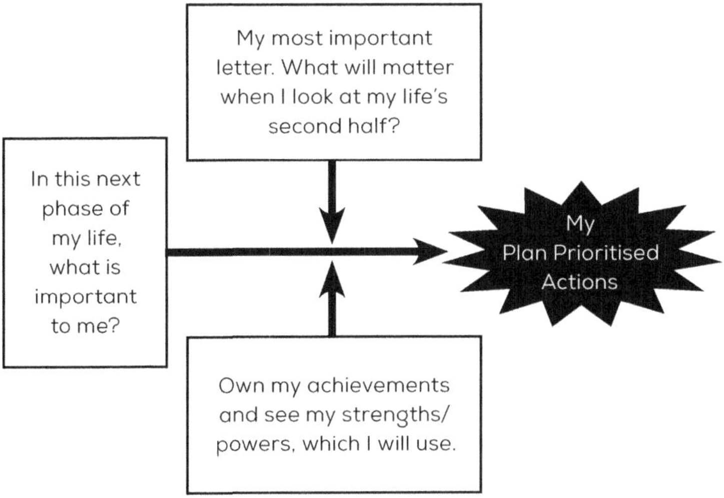

See Appendix 1 for an example.

STEP 4

LEARN FROM HOW YOU GOT HERE

I think, therefore I am.
Descartes
I think maybe a sports car would help.
Larry

At this point, provoked by the thinking you have done so far, some of you will have questions about the past.

"Why is life like this?"

"How did I get here?"

Until you get some answers, your brain may find it hard to move forward sustainably and may keep circling back. So, before you get into concrete forward planning, let's spend some time on this to release your forward journey and, indeed, to deliver some extra learnings to help. Even if you haven't started to ask questions like this, this stage will be useful, so please read on.

Everything up until now is done. You cannot undo it. You cannot change it. There are things you are happy about, that you are proud of, that worked out well or even better than you hoped. There are things that make you feel sad, that you wish hadn't happened like that, that didn't work out how you hoped. This is true for everyone. Even those people at work who seem so confident and satisfied, and definitely those people constantly posting photos of their lovely experiences on social media!

Life is not a test. It is a non-stop opportunity to learn.

The life you have lived so far has given you experiences that help shape who you are now, what you think, what you feel, and what you do. The key is to take those experiences, those perspectives, the learning and decide what you want to do with it now. You haven't crystallised. You can still flex, develop, renew, change direction, learn. Old dogs absolutely can learn new tricks. And the learning helps them feel younger.

So put simply, it can be useful to look back, but don't spend too long, don't try to change things—instead, look for the learnings. Find your strengths, and remember when you have felt powerful, potential, and fun. Harness that and go forward.

Shine your light forward. Rather than spending life's second half in the shadows of the past.

(4.1) Why is life like this?

Where does this annoying voice in the back of my mind come from?! The one that tells me

'It won't work out'

'You don't add value anymore'

'You are not good enough'

'Someone is going to find you out, any moment'

Yes, most of us have a voice that says something like this to us in our darker moments. If you have never heard a voice like this, that is great. It may still be useful to read this section to help gain more understanding about what is going on for your family members and friends.

What happens to us in the first seven years of life has a big impact on the person we become. Why?

Our brains continue to develop throughout our childhood and teenage years. In the first seven years, we have not yet developed many rational filters to what we are told or the behaviours we see role-modelled. In a way, these messages go into our heads as facts. And they sit there, unconsciously talking to us for the rest of our lives.

So it makes a difference who we spend time with during our early years, what we see them doing and hear them saying. I am not a psychologist or a psychotherapist, so I am not going to walk us down a path which others are much better qualified to guide, but my reason to raise this here is this:

Sometimes, we feel trapped or blocked by our thoughts—why do we have these thoughts that seem to get in the way? We think of tactics to get around them, we read books, and yet we still have the feeling, the nagging voice…

"Don't speak up. My thought isn't well enough thought through."

"I should know how to do that without having to ask."

"That will sound overconfident."

"They are looking at me, judging me."

We can't seem to shift these feelings, yet in the calm light of day, they are irrational. Someone else said exactly what I was thinking in the meeting, and everyone thought it was great!

The point is these feelings/voices are not rational; they were seeded in our brains before we had a chance to filter or evaluate them, and they turned into fact. Quite likely, the people who did and said the stuff, didn't mean to affect us badly. They were just doing their best.

You know, the parent who always said, *You can do better*, or when you got your school report with all As and Bs, but there was one C, they said, *what's the C doing there?*

So being loved seemed to depend on being smart.

Or some families have family myths:

"It is only worth doing if you give 110%".

"Respect your elders… speak when you are spoken to."

"If you work hard, things will work out."

"Never show weakness."

This stuff isn't true. It isn't fact. It is just someone else's view.

And some families have labels for family members, especially the children.

The lazy one, the smart one, the sensitive one, the clumsy one. Which we then do our best to live up to or disprove.

The great news is that it doesn't matter how old we are. We can still quieten this false, unhelpful voice and release ourselves. The work you are doing with this guide and the information within the guide help you make this shift.

(4.2) Being a boy

Boys grow up receiving a lot of criticism. My memory of school is that boys received a lot more criticism for their conduct than girls. They may well have earned the criticism by forgetting things, being late, not paying attention and so on. The point here is not about why it happens but a potential result. One reaction to high levels of criticism is to adapt to externalise it. i.e. to develop a mindset that *it's not me, something or someone else is causing the problem here.*

"Remember, Dad, these are my formative years. You're going to need to tread carefully here."

This experience as boys can lead to men being more resilient to criticism. Which you may think is good, and sometimes it can be useful. We've all heard the quotes about *unreasonable people doing great things and changing the world.* The problem is that it is often the criticism or developmental feedback that is most powerful and useful to hear. It is the stuff that you don't like to hear about yourself that can help you make the most important shifts in how you behave. If someone you know has something critical or developmental that they want to tell you, but you close it down, that criticism doesn't go away. The person will go and tell someone else instead about you, so actually, it gets amplified. It is always best to welcome feedback.

In the early school years, girls are often told to affiliate, to care for others, and not to stand out. We see them talk and play together in small groups. Boys, meanwhile, are often being told to get involved, compete, win, a bit of cheating is okay. (It doesn't matter if the ball was out. What matters is if the referee saw). We see boys playing sports and other active games in large groups, each boy working out where he is in the hierarchy—who can he beat, who can beat him. So, in many cases, boys don't learn much about affiliating, talking about their feelings, listening to each other. This can stay with them through life.

(4.3) It's all just chemistry

Much of what you feel is a result of the hormones (chemicals) circulating in our body. You will have heard of the human 'fright, flight, fight' response—when you encounter something scary/dangerous (fright), your body releases the hormone adrenaline, which leads to you feeling fired up, alert, and ready to either get away from the danger (flight) or to confront it (fight). Your muscles are ready to act, and you are observant of what is going on around you.

When something nice happens to you, someone pays you a compliment or perhaps your partner shoots you a sexy glance, your body releases a different hormone, dopamine, which makes you feel nice inside, positive, happy, and cuddly.

Your body releases hormones all the time, and these chemicals affect how you feel. In most cases, you are not conscious this is happening. The interesting news is that you can do things consciously to lead to particular hormones being released or not released, and thus affect your own mood. One way to do this is visualising, and I will explain how to do it in the next tools section.

(4.4) "The story of a normal guy"

Normal Guy Andrew is British. He lived his childhood in a small but comfortable house. He had a younger sister. They had their own bedrooms. His father and mother both worked. His father did longer hours. Andrew went to a local school and did well enough. He wasn't especially passionate about any subjects but was a bit better at maths and sciences. He played football and enjoyed hanging out with his friends getting around by bike. His grades were good enough to go to university.

His dad said he should study something useful, and so he studied economics. People often asked what he wanted to be, wanted to do, and he never really knew. He envied those people he met at university who knew what they wanted to do and seemed to already have a plan. Neither school nor university seemed to be much use in helping him to think through what he loved doing or might be good at doing. On leaving university, there was no question of moving back home with his parents, so he moved to Manchester and got a job. A friend was going into the sales department at a local company, and they needed another junior. So Andrew applied and got the role. His friend and he rented an apartment.

"Oh, you know how it is... Boy meets girl, boy likes girl, boy marries girl, and then 25 some years later neither of them knows what happened, who they are, or why they're here."

Andrew's twenties were fun. Work was fine—he moved roles and companies a few times. He had friends who lived in Manchester, from school and university and then also from work. Outside work, he went out with his friends—pubs and nightclubs, gigs and the occasional party. He almost always had a girlfriend. Everyone was young and doing the same sort of thing. He still played football at the weekends and occasionally tried to train more and get fit, though there never seemed to be enough time. He went home to his parents occasionally—it was always lovely to see his mum, though there wasn't much to say with his dad. He and his sister were close, but she had moved to London, so they didn't see each other a great deal. He met Kate when he was twenty-five. He got on with her friends, and she with his. Time together was easy and fun. Walking and talking, drinking coffee, long Sunday brunch… and there was lots of sex! After a few years, they decided to give it a go at living together, and that seemed to work, so they got married. Quite soon, Kate became pregnant, and their first child was born. They saved enough money for a mortgage down payment and moved into their first house.

Andrew and Kate's thirties and forties were a blur. They had a second child, bought a car, moved house a couple of times.

Andrew and Kate both worked. They tried to share looking after the children. But the reality was that Andrew did much less around the home. There was always so much to do for both of them—work, the house, the children, schools, finding some time to have some fun or relaxation. They had good local friends—other couples—they went out with occasionally for drinks or dinner. Andrew went to the pub with his mates. A holiday or maybe two each year. Andrew moved jobs a few times and became a lead salesman at a local bicycle company. He had a small team and reported to the sales director. He had clients in the UK and in other countries. He wasn't especially a cyclist, and he had never really seen himself as a salesman, but somehow, he was quite good at it, and he had a decent head for numbers and business. It didn't look likely his boss would ever leave.

Somewhere along the way, Andrew had given up football. He loved going to watch his children do sports at the weekend, and after that, there wasn't time for him to play football. It felt like there was never enough sleep. There definitely was less and less sex. Actually now, hardly any. Kate and he both loved the children. Mostly, when they were together, just the two of them, they talked about *stuff*—what had to be done, planning the week ahead. He couldn't remember when they last just walked and talked and laughed and had one of those long Sunday brunches.

Andrew had put on some weight, but was still in okay shape.

Sometimes he looked at himself in the mirror and wondered, *who are you?*

Sometimes he woke up and looked at Kate and thought *who are you?*

And then, one day, he woke up, had his shower, and after turning off the water, thought, *Is this it?*

Why this story?

Stuff happens. You do your best. You do what you think you should. Some of it works out how you wanted or expected, and some doesn't. In some aspects of your life, you didn't have a plan. You just got on with life. In other aspects, you had a plan, but the world took you down a different path—you got made redundant, someone close to you died, your wife cheated on you, and there was a pandemic. All of this happened, and it brought you here, now. You may find it hard to work out how or why your life shaped up like this. Simply accept that every experience has helped shape you. Everything that has happened has gone. What matters is what you do now, and you have the power to change the trajectory of your life's second half. You don't have to *put up with life on auto.*

STEP 5

MAKE SMALL CHANGES AND GET BIG DIFFERENCES

"Listen I'm happy you're making some positive changes, but do you have to do them all at once?"

(5.1) Clean up the basics

For most of us, some of this stuff isn't easy. But my suggestion to you is to find some areas that could do with a clean-up and some improvement and take action. You might be asking why this sort of stuff is turning up now in this guidebook. I've heard it all before. That won't make a difference.

The answer is—sometimes, in order to be able to best use the thinking tools, we need to create some mind space, some energy to help. Cleaning up our life health and wellbeing basics will help create that mind space and energy.

So, yes, you guessed it:

Don't smoke.

If you drink alcohol, drink moderately. You decide what that means—how much do you drink and still stay in charge of what you are doing, rather than the alcohol being in charge?

Drink to that point, and if you sometimes feel you need to go beyond, then so be it, but make it something unusual, not the norm.

Do some exercise, move, walk, run, swim, do squats, go to a gym, yoga, dance—anything, something. Just start and slowly build it up.

Get outside, frequently. Seeing blue sky, green grass, trees, flowers, all helps.

Get some sort of routine/ritual into your sleep.

Is it possible, for example, to sleep 11pm–7am most nights?

Get a decent pillow.

Eat more vegetables, grains and pulses.

- Carrots, broccoli, tomatoes (yes, I know that's a fruit!), green beans, courgettes
- Rice, oats, granola, porridge
- peas, lentils, chickpeas, kidney beans

Fresh, frozen, canned

You don't have to be a chef. Keep it simple. Buy a steamer to cook your vegetables. If you already have one, then get it out and use it.

Don't try everything all at once. Don't punish yourself. Do choose one or two things, and make routine changes. Stick with it. Notice the extra energy you get.

(5.2) Breathe

When you are anxious, or worried, or angry, you are less likely to make good decisions, to stay on track, to listen well, to be intentional. So what is a simple way to move yourself out of one of these fright-flight-fight states, back into a state where you can calmly decide what to do next, who to be in this moment?

Breathe.

You won't feel anxious if your heart rate is low. The easiest way to get your heart rate low, is to breathe slowly.

There are complete books about breathing and many types of breathing. I will just suggest one simple technique. Next

"OK, we'll revisit breathing another time."

time you feel yourself getting anxious or angry or in some way agitated—a red mist is coming, and perhaps you are starting not to think rationally. In your head, count one, two, three, four, five (so maybe five seconds) while you breathe in, and then the same one, two, three, four, five while you breathe out. Do it for a minute or two. Your heart rate will start to come down. Do it for another minute or two, and your heart rate should be low enough that you can start to think rationally and take back control of yourself and the situation.

You can use this technique at any time.

(5.3) Visualising

I talked earlier about a human's ability to affect the chemistry inside us (which hormones are circulating) and, therefore, how we feel. One way to do this is visualising.

Choose a positive emotion that you want to feel, for example, confident.

Close your eyes and think about a time in your life when you felt confident. Not a general time or times, an actual

"No, visualization is something else. What you're doing is spying on the neighbors."

specific moment. Maybe it was during a sports match, or when giving a presentation, or when you got a job offer after a tough interview process, or when you sat with your partner in your living room together, which you had decorated... Close your eyes and remember what you could see, who was there, what was the room like, what colours are there. What can you hear? Is the laughter, clapping, gentle chatter, maybe someone saying some specific words. What can you smell? Maybe you are outside on a summer's day, and you can smell freshly cut grass or flowers, or you are in a garage fixing your car, and you can smell car fuel.

Let yourself sink into this moment for a minute or two. And then open your eyes—how do you feel? My guess is that for sure, you feel great, and perhaps you feel a confident version of great. The amazing thing is that nothing else changed in your world in those few minutes other than you choosing what to think about and what pictures, smells, and sounds to replay in your head! And as a result, you changed your body chemistry and how you felt.

Now you know how to do this and you have a specific visualisation to go to, you can use this any time to help yourself feel more confident. For example, before an interview or a tough conversation, find somewhere quiet alone for two minutes and do your confidence visualisation. You will immediately feel better able to take on the coming situation.

And you can do it for other emotions so that you have a few to choose from, e.g. happy, loving, fierce…

(5.4) Be choiceful who you spend time with and what you spend time doing

"You are the average of the five people you spend the most time with."

JIM ROHN

Okay, yes, read it again and let it sink in. The people we spend time with have a significant effect on us. We listen to their thoughts, we see how they behave, and we edit what we say in order to fit in with them. We take their suggestions about things to do, read or listen to, places to go and visit. All of this gradually becomes part of how we think and behave. So if you spend time with people who have different values to you or who you find toxic in some way—dismissive, hard, rude—then this is affecting you. Sometimes we have to move on. People change—just because you were friends at school or college or in your first job does not mean that twenty years later, you are still a good fit as friends.

I am not suggesting that you should only choose to be friends with people who are just like you. Having friends with diverse perspectives and life experiences is great, indeed, it is a key way to keep learning and developing our own thinking and experiences. On the other hand, perhaps you spend time with people who hold opposing values to you or who have toxic behaviours, or who just don't put any effort into friendship with you. Maybe now is the moment to let them go.

Similar to the people you spend time with, what you spend your time doing, reading or watching and listening to has a big effect on what you think and feel. So, if you listen to negative and depressing news when you wake up and before you go to bed, then that probably has an effect on you. If you only ever read one type of novel, one newspaper, or watch one type of film, that has an effect on you.

Curate your time, try stuff out, and be intentional with your time and energy. Time and energy are what you have, so use it thoughtfully. Try listening to one to two different podcasts each month, swap some of that time watching TV to going for a walk or reading a book or talking with your partner. Plan in *do nothing* time. You need that, too. Sit with a coffee and just let your mind wander for twenty minutes—no phone, no paper, no computer, no list.

Specifically:

- Look back at your diary for the last couple of months: who did you spend time with, what did you spend time doing?
- Are you doing some of these things out of habit?
- If so, how can you reduce time on these things and re-route that time and energy (and perhaps money) on things you would now actively choose to do?

e.g. If you find that you are spending three hours per day either on social media or watching TV or streaming, do you really want to be spending twenty per cent of your waking time doing this? How can you half it and spend the ninety minutes you save on something you actively want to do?

From Step 5, are there some additional actions you need to take into your Plan (Step 3)? If so, go and add them now.

STEP 6

REFRESH YOUR KEY RELATIONSHIPS

To get the best form your life's second half, to live more of the life you want, it is likely that things will need to shift in the way you relate to the key people in your life. Some things you can get on with by yourself e.g. doing more exercise or taking the initiative to re-shape your role at work—great. Some other things e.g. more romantic time with my partner, more meaningful discussions with my friends, improved relationship with my father, son… require you to bring them on this journey with you.

I want to offer you two key building blocks—see love as a verb and do it more, and have better conversations with the people who are most important to you.

(6.1) Love is a verb—do it more

The greatest foundation we have, the greatest gift we can give to others, is to love and allow ourself to be loved. So, throughout your second half, find ways to feel and share love. Sometimes, for all sorts of reasons, our relationships have become less loving and more transactional. Allowing love to flourish is not some sort of magical re-discovery of what it was like. Like everything else you have worked on in this guide, it is taking practical, actionable, intentional steps to improve in the direction you want.

A key shift is to ditch the idea that love is some sort of magical thing that we fall into and out of. It is something we choose to do, that takes care and effort and time and brings great rewards.

In his book, The Road Less Travelled by M. Scott Peck, he defines love as:

"The will to extend one's self for the purpose of nurturing one's own or another's spiritual growth… Love is as love does. Love is an act of will—namely, both an intention and an action. Will also implies choice. We do not have to love. We choose to love."

"I appreciate you wanting to love more, but the heart emojis every 15 minutes have got to stop."

Bell Hooks adds in her book, All About Love:

> "To truly love, we must learn to mix ingredients—care, affection, recognition, respect, commitment, and trust, as well as open and honest communication."

If you want to refresh your loving relationships, you can. It will take some courage, care, effort and time, and it will be worth it. Don't look back and realise that you let a loving relationship slip away through tiredness or frustration or neglect.

A key to improving any relationship, including your loving relationships, is how you communicate.

(6.2) Have better conversations with the people who are most important to you

Using this guide, you have opened up new thinking for yourself, and you have started to make small changes to clean up life's basics—less beer, more vegetables, exercise three times a week. You have used the writing tools and now have a clear and actionable plan of how you want the years ahead to be. What you want to do, who you want to spend time with, how you want time to be, who you want to be. Well done. Really well done.

Now, you will almost certainly need to have better, more open, more courageous, more explorative conversations with the key people who are going to be part of that journey.

That can sound scary.

How to have better conversations?

Who to choose?

How to get started?

Who to choose?

Those people who will have a large role in your life's second half—almost certainly your partner if you have one, and perhaps there are 2-3 other really key people—close relatives and or friends.

Your Partner

First—have conversations with your partner

- Don't suddenly spring on them a new type of discussion. Let your partner know you are doing some thinking about life, how important they are to you, and how you want to find ways to talk together to look at the years ahead and how to make this a great time. Maybe let them know you found a great/simple guidebook you have been reading, which has been helping you get your thoughts clearer. Maybe your partner even gave you the book in the first place. Make it clear that you are not about to begin a big scary drama, but rather that you are feeling optimistic that you have what you hope are some useful thoughts you would like to share, and that you very much want to hear everything that they have to say. So that you can make some decisions together about how to make the years ahead great.

- Find a neutral place to go to have the discussions. e.g. go to a coffee shop. Some people like to walk together. My feeling for the early discussions is that it is important to be able to see each other's faces and body language when they are talking and listening to you. Why a neutral place? Because

"Maybe instead of saying 'bad dog' you could say 'I feel sad when you pee on the rug.'"

anywhere in your home or where you often go together will be full of memories and historic feelings that can get in the way be triggering. You want a neutral space that can help give you a feeling of safety and new beginnings/opportunities.

- Have positive intent—the whole point of talking is for the two of you together to make life's second half great for both of you. This is not a new way to try to get your partner to do what you want!
- Be ready to hear stuff you don't like.
- Be ready to say stuff you suspect your partner won't like to hear.
- Talk about all sorts of stuff—the answers from your work in this guide, the things your partner does that you love, and the things that you feel may get in the way of things being great.
- When you are talking about your partner, talk about the act—the thing she or he does or doesn't do, rather than the person, i.e. don't say you never listen to me, you don't care about me.
- Maybe do say sometimes I feel like you don't have

time to listen to me, and it makes me feel not cared for.

- The point is that she or he is still a good person, whether they have just done a great thing or a not-so-good thing. This is also a really great tip for how you talk to your children.

- Listen, listen, listen—do not react, get angry, refute. You may feel hurt or that things that are said are unfair. Do not act this out. Together, you are creating a safe space where you can both say what you need to say. For most of the stuff, actually just saying it and not being argued with, interrupted or shouted down already makes things feel better, and things that seem to be problems start to go away.

- Take turns to speak. Speak for as long as you need.

- If you ask questions, ensure those questions are to help to understand—yours and/or hers—not back-handed questions to try to prove her wrong!

- Don't try to solve things immediately. Take what you heard away with you and think about it. Don't suddenly go away and act unilaterally on it. Don't reference it sideways in day-to-day life to tweak your partner.

- At the end of each discussion, say thank you to your partner, and mean it. Ideally, say something positive about how she has behaved during the discussion, e.g., that she was brave, listened well, showed vulnerability, smiled, and cared.

- There will be many conversations together. They will get easier. This is the start of something great. In one of the conversations, when you are feeling really brave, who knows, you may even talk about sex and how to fire that up a bit.

- As a specific tip for discussing sex, a good way to find a way into this discussion could be to each do a questionnaire about the things you like or don't like and use this as a basis for discussion. It could help to break the ice. There is a good one which was published in Men's Health.*

Your Children

If you have children, then I would also suggest talking with

---

* https://www.menshealth.com/sex-women/a32147746/sex-questions-to-ask-a-girl/

each of them, but have a very different type of conversation, and with a different outcome in mind. In this case, it is simply about deepening connection and ensuring that you do not look back and wish that you had had more of a genuine relationship with these special, unique people in your lives. As before, don't just spring these conversations on your children/other close relatives. You need to give them some positive, reassuring set-up beforehand about why you want to talk.

- Travel to them.
- Talk with them like friends, not children.
- Respect them.
- Don't judge them, don't parent them, don't advise them (unless they ask).
- Ask them for their views, for their advice.
- Listen, Listen. Listen.
- Say sorry if there are things that you are sorry for.
- Let them see you cry.
- Accept their love.

"On one hand my dad has been making a lot of positive changes recently and seems really, really happy. On the other hand, that's going to be a lot to live up to."

- Give them your love unconditionally.
- Show them how to love and how to be loved.

A small group of men friends

It may be useful to develop a small group of men friends who are all up for reading this guide and using the tools and then simply come together and take time to listen to each other's answers and thinking. Just speaking this stuff out and hearing your friends' thoughts will make a big difference. You may also find common themes which you want to work on together, or you may find specific areas where one of you can help or support another in something that they want to do.

You can't cover everything in one session. Indeed, a big part of the value of a group like this is coming together every few weeks (could be face-to-face if you are lucky enough to live close together, or it could be virtually via Zoom or something equivalent). It is ideal if everyone has read the guide and gone through the stages. Then, when you are together, a simple format can be:

- Take the first minutes to arrive, and ensure everyone speaks about something—the journey here, how the week is going, yesterday's football…

- Work out how you are going to take turns doing the time-keeping
- Choose a topic from the Guide for this session, and take turns to share thoughts. Go around the group… Person one talks for up to five minutes; everyone else listens—no interruptions, no advice, no judgement. When they are finished, some of you may have a question to ask—allow another five minutes.
- Then move to the next person and do the same for them.
- When everyone has spoken, then have an open discussion exploring if there are any common themes.
- Don't try to solve things or agree on what is right or wrong. The key is simply to be able to talk, to be really listened to, and to listen to others.

So, the core dialogue each time will likely be around one of the questions or Tools / Steps in this guide. Sometimes, you may start on one question, and the energy may move to another one—that's fine.

Some other questions that can be helpful to get things moving at the beginning are:

- Something you don't know about me
- Something I love doing or used to love doing—pass time, hobby…
- Something I have done in the last three months that I am proud of
- Something about my childhood that has contributed to who I am as an adult
- Share a quote, poem, or song lyric that has meaning to me and why.

CHAPTER 7

SOME FINAL THOUGHTS

What you do now, will have a positive effect on others.

The choices you make now will enable you to make the best of your life's second half.

"When writing the story of your life,
don't let anyone else hold the pen."
JOHN KEROUAC

Live your life, not the life others think you should.

And when you make the shifts you want to make, you will naturally have a positive effect on others with whom you spend time, for example:

Your friends will start to have more open conversations and make changes for themselves.

Your partner will rediscover their mojo when they are with you.

Your children will experience greater closeness with their father, and they will see that people can keep changing throughout their life.

All these people around us, need this positivity in their lives. If you don't like the role models to which your sons are exposed, then show them a different role model, a different type of masculinity, a different way to be.

Every single positive shift you make in your life, in one of your relationships, will have a positive ripple effect for others. The power of one is great—use it.

If you would like to contact Peter to let him know how this has been for you, to share comments and suggestions or ask questions, please either email him peter@bravelyhonestlygenerously.com or connect with him on Linked In.

If you have enjoyed this book and found it useful, please do recommend it to others—write a review on the website of the book retailer where you bought it, or lend it to a friend, or give a copy to someone you love.

APPENDIX 1

EXAMPLE EXERCISES

PETER'S EXERCISES: 2012

(3.5) My achievements, and so my Strengths and Powers

Achievement (A)	What I did to make it happen (WID)
Got very good O-level results	Planned my time. Removed distractions. Still allowed myself fun and down time. Was determined.
Got good A-level results.	Did lots of practice papers. Planned my time. Stayed calm. Was very motivated and determined.
Got into my first-choice university, even after first offer looked impossible.	Trusted my intuition. Accepted my first effort wasn't going to work, so had to look for another way. Stayed positive. Didn't give up.
Stayed on at University even though I hated the first few weeks and felt really lost.	Asked for help. Gave myself time. Stayed hopeful—looked for positive signs and good people. Tried not to panic.
Left my first job after 4 years to go travelling for 10 months.	Took the risk. Was curious to learn more about the world and myself. Was courageous.
Stuck with the travel even when I was lonely or scared. As I stuck with it, it unfolded as an amazing experience full of growth and joy.	Kept moving forward. Was curious about new places and people. Was careful with money. Took some risks and grew my self-confidence.

Freshly married and with a baby on the way, we moved to China for me to do a new job.	Threw myself into the role. Kept learning. Thrived on learning about China, the culture and all the different people I worked with. Learnt what it is like to be in the minority. Stayed upbeat even when it was very challenging. Ensured that we had frequent escapes to relaxed places to decompress from tough Shanghai environment. Depended greatly on Shirley my wife.
Took one of new Global roles based in London, high on travel and on strategy development. Made a success of it.	Survived the tough physical challenge of the travel. Tough on me and on family. Accepted that life was work and family, no more, and I wasn't even contributing brilliantly to the family. Stayed focussed. Stayed optimistic even though life felt tough.
Family move to the Netherlands for a new role. First British head of marketing in this Dutch company. Did the role well, learnt Dutch, and enjoyed the Netherlands.	Took on the challenge–first time to learn and work in a new language - courage. Brought the team together in a newly formed company from merger of 2 previous companies–was constantly optimistic, and role modelled 'find a way'. Loved being in a new culture, exploring and discovering.

Organised lots of amazing family holidays.	Planning–think a year ahead. Very curious to see new places and discover them with the family. Have fun. Do it now, don't wait.
Maintained best University friendships.	Focussed on a few people. Kept in touch. Find reasons to get together–make stuff happen.
Took mum on annual mini-holidays until she became too frail to travel.	Made this happen, even though not asked or always easy. Determined, focussed, caring.
Led Vitality for Unilever first as VP and then as SVP, in total for 5 years. From a time when few believed, through to the time it became the core of the company strategy / purpose - Unilever Sustainable Living Plan.	Courage, taking the risk to go into a completely new work arena. Led transformation from the front. Brought energy, optimism, belief and business rationale for change. Kept moving forward–find a way.
Made great new friends when we eventually settled in the UK.	Allowed myself to be me - the good, the fun and the annoying. Made social activities happen–plan and organise. Bring energy.
Accepted my spinal scoliosis and learnt how to manage it.	Accept in life I have to play the cards I am dealt; some things can't be undone. Be optimistic. Found a way, asking questions, getting support, trying stuff out e.g. yoga.

Looking at my achievements and what I did to make them happen, the themes—my key strengths/powers are:

- Determination—turn up, get stuff done, see things through.
- Curiosity about people and the world.
- Optimism—believe things can be better, try to make it so, bring positive energy.
- Courage—try new things—jobs, countries, friendships, be excited by a blank sheet of paper.
- Planning—methodical, make a plan, follow the plan.

(3.6) In this next phase of my life, what is important to me?

Turn the top 5 items into priorities for action:

- Am I doing enough to make this happen?
- What is getting in the way? How to reduce the barrier?
- Who can help? What can help?
- Make my plan.

1) Maintain my health as the foundation to deliver everything else.

- Need to find role(s) for coming years with much less travel and jet lag
- Try to reduce and better organise business travel in the short term
- Reduce alcohol consumption
- Stretch every morning and do yoga at least three times a week

2) Keep the family home where we are—schools, friends, life.

- This depends on (1) and (3)

3) Earn £xyz/year for three to four years.

- Land my next role
- Progress internal discussions for opportunities
- Update my CV and start talking with Exec Searchers re external opportunities
- Use my network—start talking to people

4) Develop a plan for what my work life will be for the 10 years after my next & final corporate role

- Explore coaching—what, where to train, how to get started
- Identify people I know who are experienced in this space and can help me understand and explore

5) Ensure I have enough good time (be present & have energy) with the boys

- Be better at unstructured time, just being together
- Listen more, give less advice!
- When I land my next role, could I negotiate time out (?6 months) between roles to really decompress and be present?

6) Give enough focus—time, energy, thought to my relationship with my wife Shirley

- How to really create fun, romantic time rather than just doing the transactional stuff that needs to happen to make life work?

7) My next job to be in a company whose values I share and brands I care about.

8) My next job to be in the leadership team, at the heart of the company's way forward.

9) Continue to have mini holidays with mum for as long as possible.

10) My next job to be in a company with an authentic sustainable purpose.

11) Have lovely warm summer family holidays for as long as we can.

12) Improve my cardio fitness and muscular strength.

PETER, 2032

(3.7) The most important Letter - to myself

I am sitting on the terrace of an Italian villa. The sky is blue, and the air is soft and fragrant. The terrace has a view of the sea in one direction, and there are lots of green plants and trees around the villa. I am calm, breathing deeply & slowly, smiling.

We are about to have a long lazy lunch with the family—Shirley, our boys and their loved ones. I feel so much love and so much gratitude. I am also genuinely excited, as I always am, about the simple, tasty food and wine here in Italy.

Tomorrow, we will be joined by our closest friends to do it all again, through the afternoon and into the evening. We will stay for the week, and everyone has their own plans to be together as much or as little as they want.

I have always dreamt of being able to make this happen and to be able to relax into myself to, enjoy it fully, be really present.

And how has been the last twenty years?

I am here, and I have my health, so I guess that's a good start. Shirley and I are together, and the boys have good lives with loving partners and great friends.

Not everything went as I tried to make it happen, but I guess that is life, and the important stuff did go well.

I completed my corporate career nicely, continued to train and develop my coaching skills, and set up my coaching practice. The first two years were tough, developing a client base and my true sense of self as a coach. There were times I thought it wouldn't work, but I stayed calm and received great support from my mentors. That gave me the confidence I needed. I am still coaching, and I love it. Working with diverse leaders to develop themselves, achieve their goals and create inclusive, powerful teams brings me great joy and constant expansion of my perspective and learning. Out of the coaching came my book, which has been an amazing experience and, once again, brought me to meet many new and interesting people.

I got well enough on top of my health and fitness. Yoga was life-changing. Quarterly visit to my chiropractor wizard. I was never able to do the amount or type of walks many of my friends do. I guess that is a combination of the innate weakness in my back, and I guess it just was never important enough to me! We are so lucky that we can eat healthily. Wine continues to be a joy and a weakness. Plus ça change...

The financial Excel sheet of life worked out okay, which meant we could stay in the house we bought back in the UK in 2005. I love that house. So many great memories of parties and dinners, the boys and their friends around the kitchen island—still happening. And, of course, I have many memories of the spaniels—those big brown eyes full of love every morning, lifting my spirits. And the acceptance of the never-ending dog hair, winter mud and begrudging rainy dog walks.

Shirley and I have had our ups and downs, but she has been and is still my beautiful creative, and fun life partner. She makes me smile, she keeps me in the present, and along the way, we made our big decisions together. She is still elegant and sexy. My life would have been so much less without her.

I hope I got things right enough with the boys. They are kind capable, loving men. I am super proud of them. In these later years, I tried to be present and available for them in whatever way was most useful for them, as opposed to what worked for me. That has always been a challenge for me. I always have views, ideas, questions, thoughts, and worries; keeping them in my head and not pressing them onto the boys was always a challenge. Remember Peter—it is not your life, it is theirs. They seem happy and fulfilled, which is all that matters. And they are here today, so lucky me.

I have been fortunate, too, to have a few wonderful friends. I focussed my time and friendship energy on a few, and I believe that was a good decision. We never get bored. Instead, we just keep uncovering new layers of friendship and fun. Most of them will be here tomorrow. As the years unfolded, I became more and more relaxed and able to find myself with them. Dinners, holidays, pub nights, shared garden projects…

I always said that worry and regret are useless. I reduced my worry, though I never fully silenced it. I hate the idea of regret and am not going to give it a voice here in this letter.

So, what did I learn?

- Love and be loved.
- Be kind.

- Be optimistic.
- Be determined—back yourself.
- Be present.
- Have fun.
- Drop toxic relationships.
- Invest time in good people. Turn up for them when you are needed, not just when you are asked.
- Ask great questions and listen to the answers.
- Do yoga.

And what next?

A few more years would be nice. To live in our home until the end. Not be a burden to anyone as age creeps in. Be present and grateful and full of love today and tomorrow. And if the day after that was it, then it has been a good ride.

(3.8) Use your possibility building blocks to build your plan

Use the actions coming from 'What is important to me' as the basis for the weeks, months and perhaps one to five years ahead. From your most important letter add in anything more or perhaps cut out something that really isn't as important as you thought. Keep your list of strengths and look at it every few weeks, to remind yourself to use your powers to live the life you want. Perhaps you can add into your some of your actions how you will use your strengths to get the outcomes you want.

Don't try to do everything. Focus on the top priorities. Perhaps do some phasing—start some things now and others in a year's time.

Peter's plan, 2012

Use my strengths: Be Optimistic and Determined, back myself. Make this plan, make it feel positive, it will change, but I have done all this work to get to this plan, so it is worth following through on it. No one else can make this happen.

Next 6 months

1) Land my next role

- Progress internal discussions for opportunities
- Update my CV and start talking with Exec Searchers re external opportunities
- Use my network—start talking to people

If I move companies, ideally, I will be able to have some time out between roles.

2) Ensure I have enough good time (be present & have energy) with the boys

- Be better at unstructured time, just being together
- Listen more, ask good questions rather than have my own answers.

Take them to sports and drama. Watching films together is okay... Be 100% present at meal times.

3) Find some health step-ups

- Reduce and better organise business travel as much as feasible
- Try drinking alcohol only two nights per week
- Stretch every morning and try out yoga at local place
- When I do travel, take gym kit and use hotel gym

6–24 months—headlines

Flesh out actions more when I get there, plus use learning from six months coming.

4) Start my new role and make a success of it

- Remember to make a 100 days plan

5) Make time for Shirley and me

- Date night at least once per month
- Can we find a shared activity to do together—dancing, tennis?

6) Develop a plan for what my work life will be for the 10 years after this next and final corporate role

- Explore coaching—what, where to train, how to get started
- Identify people I know who are experienced in this space and can help me understand and explore.

7) Continue with yoga and add some more committed cardio fitness—try boxercise?

8) Plan nice stuff

- family holidays
- something with local friends once a month
- something with university friends 2-3 times a year

2–5 years

9) Finish up corporate work life & transition into next phase

- If coaching is the direction, then immerse, do more training, and learn how to develop a coaching business

- get finances in order
- work with Shirley on this—how will life be like for her if I am working from home, what do I need to be mindful of…

10) Find how to make the best of the coming years with Mum & Dad

Note: Use whatever format is best for you for your plan. A list like this works for me. You may prefer a table or a mind map. It can be useful to put specific timings for some actions especially the closer in ones, in order to generate momentum. e.g. within one week, within four weeks.

ACKNOWLEDGEMENTS

Mark Anderson for his wonderful cartoons and his partnership in creating the unique humanity of this guide.

Steve Kuhn for his calm creative craftmanship and vision, taking the raw materials and bringing them to life.

Through my life, many people have supported, helped and believed in me—giving me the strength and opportunities to take on challenges and learn. I would like to acknowledge a few.

Mr. Hicks, my year tutor at the Broxbourne School, who calmed me when I tried to leave Cambridge University two weeks in.

Vindi Banga, Ralph Kugler, Roger Kirman and Thomas Derville, who inspired and mentored me during my years at Unilever.

Kevin Greenleaves, my coach and later coaching mentor, whose professional wisdom helped me unlock a next chapter of life.

Dave Sellers & Darren Coles who taught me Neuro Linguistic Programming, which opened for me a new world of understanding communication.

Nick Craig, Katherine Tulpa and Ann James, 3 wonderful coaches, whose belief in me as a coach gave me much needed confidence.

Shirley my life partner, who makes me smile and reminds me to enjoy life rather than organise it.

Will and Hugo who inspire me and are full of love.

Printed in Great Britain
by Amazon

34297036R00078